Defense of the Bible as a Schoolbook

Dr. Benjamin Rush

Edited and Introduced by
Stephen A. Flick, Ph.D.

Christian Heritage Press

Defense of the Bible
As a Schoolbook

Dr. Benjamin Rush

Published by:
Christian Heritage Fellowship, Inc.
1121 N. Charles G. Seivers Blvd, #143
Clinton, TN 37717

Cover Design: Stephen A. Flick

ISBN-13: 9781796221084

Printed in USA

The ministry of Christian Heritage Fellowship, Inc. is made possible through the generous contributions of friends who seek to promote America's Christian heritage. Your contribution will enable us to continue to reclaim our Christian heritage for succeeding generations. You may contribute at the following web page:

https://christianheritagefellowship.com/donate

Dedicated to
Isaac, Joshua, Gabriel,
Seth, Arianna, and Sarah Beth
February 2, 2019

Special appreciation is extended to Beth Bagby for her assistance in the preparation of this manuscript.

Contents

The Foundation of American Education

A Brief Summary

It is a surprise to most Americans to realize that the United States Supreme Court acknowledged the rightful place of the Bible in America's schoolrooms. While most are aware of the June 17, 1963 Supreme Court 8-1 ruling against Bible reading in public schools (*Abington School District v. Schempp*), the rightful place of the Bible in the schoolrooms of America was asserted soon after the arrival of the Pilgrims and Puritans in the New World. From the origin of public education—as early as the 1640's—until 1947 and following, prayer and Bible reading was a part of American classrooms. Beginning in the late 1940's, liberal judges began their attack upon this three-hundred-year practice—a practice supported by law and court decisions!

EARLIEST SCHOOL LAWS AND THE BIBLE

The earliest school laws in colonial America were formulated in Massachusetts during the 1640's. Many of the Christian immigrants to America—along with their spiritual forefathers—had been persecuted in the Old World. Sadly, many of their persecutors themselves had claimed to be Christians. But, American immigrants believed that because the Bible had not been translated into the mother tongue of European inhabitants, their persecutors were often unaware that their atrocities and brutality violated the will of God as disclosed in the Bible.

In the early set of Massachusetts' school laws, the General School Law of 1647 specifically addressed the importance of Bible reading in public schools. To prevent society from being corrupted by "that old deluder Satan" and "saint-seeming deceivers," Massachusetts proposed that students possess a knowledge of the Scriptures in their mother tongue to avoid the repetition of the atrocities that occurred in Europe:

> It being one chief project of that old deluder, Satan, to keep men from the knowledge of the Scriptures, as in former times by keeping them in an unknown tongue, so in these latter times by persuading from the use of tongues, that so that at least the true sense and meaning of the original might be clouded and corrupted with love and false glosses of saint-seeming deceivers; and to the end that learning may not be buried in the grave of our forefathers, in church and commonwealth, the Lord assisting our endeavors.[1]

The 1844 Supreme Court

Stephen Girard was a French-born banker who became a naturalized American citizen following the American Revolution. During the War of 1812, Girard saved the United States government from financial collapse and is believed to be one of the wealthiest people in American history. Initially, he earned his fortune in trade. Though never owning more than six ships at any time, he purchased a total of eighteen ships during his career, the best of which he named after the French irreligious infidels, Montesquieu, Rousseau, Voltaire.[2] Girard bequeathed nearly his entire fortune to both municipal and charitable institutions in New Orleans and Philadelphia—the latter city being where he resided. As an atheist, Girard sought to advance his irreligion in the youth of Philadelphia by giving two million dollars[3] of his estate to begin a school for boys which disallowed any opportunity for Christian influence. In his will, he stated,

> I enjoin and require that no ecclesiastic, mission-ary, or minister of any sect whatsoever, shall ever hold or exercise any station or duty whatever in the said college; nor shall any such person ever be admit-ted for any purpose, or as a visitor, within the prem-ises appropriated to the purposes of the said college...[4]

Consistent with the understanding that the Bible was the source ca-pable of producing the greatest good in society, the Supreme Court in 1844 ruled that the Bible should not be excluded from American classrooms. As was true for the General School Law of 1647, the Supreme Court Justices believed the Bible exercised the greatest good in society. Writing the unanimous opinion for the Court was Justice Joseph Story:

> Why may not the Bible, and especially the New Testament, without note or comment, be read and taught as a divine revelation in the college —— its general precepts expound-ed, its evidences explained, and its glorious principles of morality inculcated? What is there to prevent a work, not sectarian, upon the general evidences of Christianity, from being read and taught in the college by lay teachers?

> ...Where can the purest principles of morality be learned so clearly or so perfectly as from the New Testament? Where are benevolence, the love of truth, sobriety, and industry, so pow-erfully and irresistibly inculcated as in the sacred volume?[5]

INTRODUCTION TO DR. BENJAMIN RUSH

On April 19, 1813, Dr. Benjamin Rush—one of America's Founding Fathers—passed into eternity at the age of sixty-seven. Along with George Washington and Benjamin Franklin, Benjamin Rush was regarded as one of the three most important Founding Fathers of America.[6] Though secularists incorrectly take advantage of Benja-min Franklin's and Thomas Jefferson's alleged rejection of Christianity, there is no opportunity for misinterpretation concerning one of the godliest and most deeply dedicated Christians among America's Founding Fathers, Dr. Benjamin Rush.

Dr. Benjamin Rush
JANUARY 4, 1746 – APRIL 19, 1813

– BY CHARLES WILLSON PEALE

Rush was one of three of the most important Founding Fathers. Resident of Philadelphia, he was a physician, politician, social reformer, humanitarian, and educator. He signed the Declaration of Independence and was Surgeon General of the Continental Army.

Dr. Rush is remembered as the "Father of American Medicine,"[7] and "The Father of Public Schools Under the Constitution."[8] As one of the first organizers of America's first anti-slavery society,[9] he soon became a leader in the national abolition effort—a movement primarily dominated by Christians.[10]

Jacob Duché
1737–1798

– BY MAX ROSENTHAL

Duche was the pastor of Christ Church in Philadelphia, Pennsylvania. Because of the important role Christ Church occupied in America's bid for freedom, it was called the "Nation's Church." Duche's first prayer in Congress is capture in an historic painting by that name.

It is not true that America was founded upon irreligious secularism, but rather upon the influence of Christianity. The single greatest reason that America's Founding Fathers did not employ much religious or Christian terminology in national or federal legislation is because of the diversity of Christian opinions that existed among them. This fact is very evident from the very First Continental Congress when delegates were establishing the procedures and protocols of Congress. On the second day of Congress, Samuel Adams, "Father of the American Revolution, said "he was no bigot [or denominational partisan], and could hear a prayer from any gentleman of piety and virtue, who was at the same time a friend to his country," and then proceeded to nominate Rev. Jacob Duché to open Congress with prayer. Following this suggestion, the Continental Congress offered the following resolution: "Resolved, That the Revd. Mr. Duché be desired to open the Congress tomorrow morning with prayers, at the Carpenter's Hall, at 9 o'clock."[11] Rev. Duche was the Anglican rector or pastor at Christ Church—"The Nation's Church"—and became Congress' first chaplain. Though eleven of the thirteen states originally had state churches, delegates to Congress as early as 1774 realized that hope of a unified national government would be dashed if any one denomination was perceived as dominating the entire nation.

Yet, America's Founding Fathers understood that Christian morality was necessary to good government. Congress issued prayer, thanksgiving, and fasting proclamations during and after the Revolution, when America had been established under the United States Constitution. The Founding Fathers understood that Christian morals and values alone could sustain America. One of the greatest demonstrations of this fact is provided in the following brief essay by Dr. Rush titled, *A Defense of the Use of the Bible as a Schoolbook, Addressed To The Rev. Jeremy Belknap, Of Boston*.

Rev. Jeremy Belknap
JUNE 4, 1744 – JUNE 20, 1798

– BY HENRY SARGENT

Rev. Belknap was an American clergyman and historian. After the Battle of Lexington (1775), he became a chaplain to units of the Dover militia during the Siege of Boston, remaining with his New Hampshire troops throughout the winter.

Because early America had very active ministers who believed King George III had violated God's law, they called for revolt against the King. For nearly a decade, ministers preached about ways that the

King was violating the law of God as revealed in the Bible. Rev. Jeremy Belknap was among those ministers who taught that the King was violating God's laws in the way he was seeking to govern the American Colonies. In 1767, Rev. Belknap became the pastor of the Congregational Church in Dover, New Hampshire. Eight years later, in 1775, some units of the Dover militia were activated following the Battle of Lexington to support the American cause in the Siege of Boston. Rev. Belknap accompanied those militia units to Boston as chaplain to the New Hampshire troops engaged in the siege and remained with them through the next winter. It was to his friend, Rev. Belknap, that Dr. Rush addressed his essay concerning the need for America's youth to be trained in the teachings of the Bible. That essay is presented below in its entirety and reflects not only the academic convictions of the clergy, but the concern of America's Founding Fathers, among whom Dr. Rush was among the most highly esteemed.

A Defense of the Use of the Bible as a Schoolbook

Addressed to the Rev. Jeremy Belknap, of Boston

DEAR SIR,

It is now several months, since I promised to give you my reasons for preferring the Bible as a schoolbook, to all other compositions. I shall not trouble you with an apology for my delaying so long to comply with my promise, but shall proceed immediately to the subject of my letter.

Before I state my arguments in favor of teaching children to read by means of the Bible, I shall assume the five following propositions.

I. That Christianity is the only true and perfect religion, and that in proportion as mankind adopt its principles, and obey its precepts, they will be wise, and happy.

II. That a better knowledge of this religion is to be acquired by reading the Bible, than in any other way.

III. That the Bible contains more knowledge necessary to man in his present state, than any other book in the world.

IV. That knowledge is most durable, and religious instruction most useful, when imparted in early life,

V. That the Bible, when not read in schools, is seldom read in any subsequent period of life.

ARGUMENTS IN FAVOR OF THE USE OF THE BIBLE

My arguments in favor of the use of the Bible as a schoolbook are founded,

I. In the constitution of the human mind.

1. The memory is the first faculty which opens in the minds of children. Of how much consequence, then, must it be, to impress it with the great truths of Christianity, before it is pre-occupied with less interesting subjects! As all liquors, which are poured into a cup generally taste of that which first filled it, so all the knowledge, which is added to that which is treasured up in the memory from the Bible, generally receives an agreeable and useful tincture from it.

2. There is a peculiar aptitude in the minds of children for religious knowledge. I have constantly found them in the first six or seven years of their lives, more inquisitive upon religious subjects, than upon any others: and an ingenious instructor of youth has informed me, that he has found young children more capable of receiving just ideas upon the most difficult tenets of religion, than upon the most simple branches of human knowledge. It would be strange if it were otherwise; for God creates all his means to suit all his ends. There must of course be a fitness between the human mind, and the truths which are essential to its happiness.

3. The influence of prejudice is derived from the impressions, which are made upon the mind in early life; prejudices are of two kinds, true and false. In a world where false prejudices do so much mischief, it would discover great weakness not to oppose them, by such as are true.

I grant that many men have rejected the prejudices derived from the Bible: but I believe no man ever did do, without having been made wiser of better, by the early operation of these prejudices upon his mind. Every just principle that is to be found in the writings of Voltaire, is borrowed from the Bible: and the morality of the

Deists, which has been so much admired and praised, is, I believe, in most cases, the effect of habits, produced by early instruction in the principles of Christianity.

4. We are subject, by a general law in our natures, to what is called habit. Now if the study of the scriptures be necessary to our happiness at any time of our lives, the sooner we begin to read them, the more we shall be attached to them; for it is peculiar to all the acts of habit, to become easy, strong and agreeable by repetition.

5. It is a law in our natures, that we remember longest the knowledge we acquire by the greatest number of our senses. Now a knowledge of the contents of the Bible, is acquired in school by the aid of the eyes and the ears; for children after getting their lessons, always say them to their masters in an audible voice; of course there is a presumption, that this knowledge will be retained much longer than if it had been acquired in any other way.

6. The interesting events and characters, recorded and described in the Old and New Testaments, are accommodated above all others to seize upon all the faculties of the minds of children. The understanding, the memory, the imagination, the passions, and the moral powers, are all occasionally addressed by the various incidents which are contained in those divine books, insomuch that not to be delighted with them, is to be devoid of every principle of pleasure that exists in a sound mind.

7. There is a native love of truth in the human mind. Lord Shaftsbury says, that "truth is so congenial to our minds, that we love even the shadow of it:" and Horace, in his rules for composing an epic poem, establishes the same law in our natures, by advising the "fictions in poetry to resemble truth." Now the Bible contains more truths than any other book in the world: so true is the testimony that it bears of God in his works of creation, providence, and redemption, that it is called truth itself, by way of preeminence above things that are only simply true. How forcibly are we struck with the evidences of truth, in the history of the Jews, above what we discover in the history of other nations? Where do we find a hero, or an historian record his own faults or vices except in the Old Tes-

tament? Indeed, my friend, from some accounts which I have read of the American Revolution, I begin to grow skeptical to all history except to that which is contained in the Bible. Now if this book be known to contain nothing but what is materially true, the mind will naturally acquire a love for it from this circumstance: and from this affection for the truth in other books, and a preference of it in all the transactions of life.

8. There is a wonderful property in the memory, which enables it in old age, to recover the knowledge it had acquired in early life, after it had been apparently forgotten for forty or fifty years. Of how much consequence, then, must it be, to fill the mind with that species of knowledge, in childhood and youth, which, when recalled in the decline of life, will support the soul under the infirmities of age, and smooth the avenues of approaching death? The Bible is the only book which is capable of affording this support to old age; and it is for this reason that we find it resorted to with so much diligence and pleasure by such old people as have read it in early life. I can recollect many instances of this kind in persons who discovered no attachment to the Bible, in the meridian of their lives, who have notwithstanding, spent the evening of them, in reading no other book. The late Sir John Pringle, Physician to the Queen of Great Britain, after passing a long life in camps and at court, closed it by studying the scriptures. So anxious was he to increase his knowledge in them that he wrote to Dr. Michaelis, a learned professor of divinity in Germany, for an explanation of a difficult text of scripture, a short time before his death.

II. My second argument in favor of the use of the Bible in schools, is founded upon an implied command of God, and upon the practice of several of the wisest nations of the world.-In the 6th chapter of Deuteronomy, we find the following words, which are directly to my purpose,

> "And thou shalt love the Lord thy God, with all thy heart and with all thy soul, and with all thy might. And these words which I command thee this day shall be in thine heart. And thou shalt teach them diligently unto thy children, and shalt talk of them when thou sit-

test in thine house, and when thou walkest by the way, and when thou liest down, and when thou risest up."

It appears, moreover, from the history of the Jews, that they flourished as a nation, in proportion as they honored and read the books of Moses, which contained, a written revelation of the will of God, to the children of men. The law was not only neglected, but lost during the general profligacy of manners which accompanied the long and wicked reign of Manasseh. But the discovery of it, in the rubbish of the temple, by Josiah, and its subsequent general use, were followed by a return of national virtue and prosperity. We read further, of the wonderful effects which the reading of the law by Ezra, after his return from his captivity in Babylon, had upon the Jews. They hung upon his lips with tears, and showed the sincerity of their repentance, by their general reformation.

The learning of the Jews, for many years consisted in nothing but a knowledge of the scriptures. These were the text books of all the instruction that was given in the schools of their prophets. It was by means of this general knowledge of their law, that those Jews that wandered from Judea into our countries, carried with them and propagated certain ideas of the true God among all the civilized nations upon the face of the earth. And it was from the attachment they retained to the Old Testament, that they procured a translation of it into the Greek language, after they lost the Hebrew tongue, by their long absence from their native country. The utility of this translation, commonly called the Septuagint, in facilitating the progress of the gospel, is well known to all who are acquainted with the history of the first age of the Christian church.

But the benefits of an early and general acquaintance with the Bible, were not confined only to the Jewish nations. They have appeared in many countries in Europe, since the reformation. The industry, and habits of order, which distinguish many of the German nations, are derived from their early instruction in the principles of Christianity, by means of the Bible. The moral and enlightened character of the inhabitants of Scotland, and of the New England States, appears to be derived from the same cause. If we descend from nations to sects, we shall find them wise and prosperous in proportion as they become early acquainted with the scriptures. The Bible is still used as a schoolbook among the Quakers. The morality of this sect of Christians is universally acknowledged. Nor is this all; their prudence in the management of their private affairs, is as much a mark of their society, as their sober manners.

I wish to be excused for repeating here, that if the Bible did not convey a single direction for the attainment of future happiness, it should be read in our schools in preference to all other books, from its containing the greatest portion of that kind of knowledge which is calculated to produce private and public temporal happiness.

We err not only in human affairs, but in religion likewise, only because "we do not know the scriptures." The opposite systems of the numerous sects of Christians arise chiefly from their being more instructed in catechisms, creeds, and confessions of faith, than in the scriptures. Immense truths, I believe, are concealed in them. The time, I have no doubt, will come, when posterity will view and pity our ignorance of these truths, as much as we do the ignorance of the disciples of our Savior, who knew nothing of the meaning of those plain passages in the Old Testament which were daily fulfilling before their eyes. Whenever that time shall arrive, those truths which have escaped our notice, or if discovered, have been thought to be opposed to each other, or to be inconsistent with themselves, will then like the stones of Solomon's temple, be found so exactly to accord with each other, that they shall be cemented without noise or force, into one simple and sublime system of religion.

But further, we err, not only in religion but in philosophy likewise, because we "do not know or believe "the scriptures." The sciences have been compared to a circle of which religion composes a part. To understand any one of them perfectly it is necessary to have some knowledge of them all. Bacon, Boyle, and Newton included the scriptures in the inquiries to which their universal geniuses disposed them, and their philosophy was aided by their knowledge in them. A striking agreement has been lately discovered between the history of certain events recorded in the Bible and some of the operations and productions of nature, particularly those which are related in Whitehurst's observations on the deluge, in Smith's account of the origin of the variety of color in the human species, and in Bruce's travels. It remains yet to be shown how many other events, related in the Bible, accord with some late important discoveries in the principles of medicine. The events, and the principles alluded to, mutually establish the truth of each other. From the discoveries of the Christian philosophers, whose names have been last mentioned, I have been led to question whether most harm has been done to revelation, by those divines who have unduly multiplied the objects of faith, or by those deists who have unduly multiplied the objects of reason, in explaining the scriptures.

ANSWERING OBJECTIONS

I shall now proceed to answer some of the objections which have been made to the use of the Bible as a schoolbook.

I. We are told, that the familiar use of the Bible in our schools, has a tendency to lessen a due reverence for it. This objection, by proving too much, proves nothing at all. If familiarity lessens respect for divine things, then all those precepts of our religion, which enjoin the daily or weekly worship of the Deity, are improper. The Bible was not intended to represent a Jewish ark; and it is an anti-Christian idea, to suppose that it can be profaned, by being carried into a schoolhouse, or by being handled by children. But where will the Bible be read by young people with more reverence than in a school? Not in most private families; for I believe there are few parents, who preserve so much order in their houses, as is kept in our common English schools.

II. We are told, that there are many passages in the Old Testament, that are improper to be read by children, and that the greatest part of it is no way interesting to mankind under the present dispensation of the gospel. There are I grant, several chapters, and many verses in the Old Testament, which in their present unfortunate translation, should be passed over by children. But I deny that any of the books of the Old Testament are not interesting to mankind, under the gospel dispensation. Most of the characters, events, and ceremonies, mentioned in them, are personal, providential, or instituted types of the Messiah: All of which have been, or remain yet to be, fulfilled by him. It is from an ignorance or neglect of these types, that we have so many deists in Christendom; for so irrefragably do they prove the truth of Christianity, that I am sure a young man who had been regularly instructed in their meaning, could never doubt afterwards of the truth of any of its principles. If any obscurity appears in these principles, it is only (to use the words of the poet) because they are dark, with excessive bright.

I know there is an objection among many People to teach children doctrines of any kind, because they are liable to be controverted. But where will this objection lead us? The being of a God, and the obligations of morality, have both been controverted; and yet who has objected to our teaching these doctrines to our children?

The curiosity and capacities of young people for the mysteries of religion, awaken much sooner than is generally supposed. Of this we have two remarkable proofs in the Old Testament. The first is mentioned in the twelfth chapter of Exodus:

> And it shall come when your children shall say unto you, "What mean you by this service?" that ye shall say, "It is the sacrifice of the Lord's Passover, who passed over the houses of Israel in Egypt, when he smote the Egyptians, and delivered our houses." And the children of the Israel went away, and did as the Lord had commanded Moses and Aaron.

A second proof of the desire of children to be instructed in the mysteries of religion, is found in the sixth chapter of Deuteronomy.

> And when thy son asketh thee in the time to come saying, "What mean the testimonies and the statutes and the judgements which the Lord our God hath commanded you?" Then thou shalt say unto they son, "We were Pharoah's bondmen in Egypt, and the Lord our God brought us out of Egypt with a mighty hand."

These enquiries from the mouths of children are perfectly natural; for where is the parent who has not had similar questions proposed to him by his children upon their being first conducted to a place of worship, and upon their beholding, for the first time, either of the sacraments of our religion?

Let us not be wiser than our Maker. If moral precepts alone could have reformed mankind, the mission of the Son of God into our world, would have been unnecessary. He came to promulgate a system of doctrines, as well as a system of morals. The perfect morality of the gospel rests upon a doctrine, which, though often controverted, has never been refuted, I mean the vicarious life and death of the Son of God. This sublime and ineffable doctrine delivers us from the absurd hypotheses of modern philosophers, concerning the foundation of moral obligation, and fixes it upon the eternal and self-moving principle of LOVE. It concentrates a whole system of ethics in a single text of scripture: "A new commandment I give unto you, that ye love one another, even as I have loved you." By withholding the knowledge of this doctrine from children, we deprive ourselves of the best means of awakening moral sensibility in their minds. We do more, we furnish an argument, for withholding from them a knowledge of the morality of the gospel likewise; for this, in many instances, is as supernatural, and therefore as liable to be controverted, as any of the doctrines or miracles which are mentioned in the New Testament. The miraculous conception of the Savior of the world by a virgin, is not more opposed to the ordinary course of natural events, nor is the doctrine of the atonement more above human reason, than those moral precepts, which command us to love our enemies, or to die for our friends.

III. It has been said, that the division of the Bible into chapters and verses, renders it more difficult to be read, by children than many other books.

By a little care in a master, this difficulty may be obviated, and even an advantage derived from it. It may serve to transfer the attention of the scholar to the sense of a subject; and no person will ever read well, who is guided by any thing else, in his stops, emphasis, or accents. The division of the Bible into chapters and verses, is not a greater obstacle to its being read with ease, than the bad punctuation of most other books. I deliver this stricture upon other books, from the authority of Mr. Rice, the celebrated author of the art of speaking, whom I heard declare in a large company in London, that he had never seen a book properly pointed in the English Language. He exemplified, notwithstanding, by reading to the same company a passage from Milton, his perfect knowledge of the art of reading.

Some people, I know, have proposed to introduce extracts from the Bible, into our schools, instead of the Bible itself. Many excellent works of this kind, are in print, but if we admit any one of them, we shall have the same inundation of them that we have had of grammars, spelling books, and lessons for children, many of which are published for the benefit of the authors only, and all of them have tended greatly to increase the expense of education. Besides, these extracts or abridgements of the Bible, often contain the tenets of particular sects or persons, and therefore, may be improper for schools composed of the children of different sects of Christians. The Bible is a cheap book, and is to be had in every bookstore. It is, moreover, esteemed and preferred by all sects; because each finds its peculiar doctrines in it. It should therefore be used in preference to any abridgements of it, or histories extracted from it.

I have heard it proposed that a portion of the Bible should be read every day by the master, as a means of instructing children in it: But this is a poor substitute for obliging children to read it as a schoolbook; for by this means we insensibly engrave, as it were, its contents upon their minds: and it has been remarked that children, instructed in this way in the scriptures, seldom forget any part of them. They have the same advantage over those persons, who have only heard the scriptures read by a master, that a man who has worked with the tools of the mechanical employment for several years, has over the man who has only stood a few hours in a work shop and seen the same business carried on by other people.

In this defense of the use of the Bible as a schoolbook, I beg you would not think that I suppose the Bible to contain the only revelation which God has made to man. I believe in an internal revelation, or a moral principle, which God has implanted in the heart of every man, as the precursor of his final dominion over the whole human race. How much this internal revelation accords with the external, remains yet to be explored by philosophers. I am disposed to believe, that most of the doctrines of Christianity revealed in the Bible might be discovered by a close examination of all the principles of action in man: But who is equal to such an enquiry? It certainly does not suit the natural indolence, or laborious employments of a great majority of mankind. The internal revelation of the gospel may be compared to the straight line which is made through the wilderness by the assistance of a compass, to a distant country, which few are able to discover, while the Bible resembles a public road to the same country, which is wide, plain, and easily found. "And a highway shall be there, and it shall be called the way of holiness. The way faring men, though fools, shall not err therein."

Neither let me in this place exclude the Revelation which God has made of himself to man in the works of creation. I am far from wishing to lessen the influence of this species of Revelation upon mankind. But the knowledge of God obtained from this source, is obscure and feeble in its operation, compared with that which is derived from the Bible. The visible creation speaks of the Deity in hieroglyphics, while the Bible describes all his attributes and perfections in such plain, and familiar language that "he who runs may read."

How kindly has our maker dealt with his creatures, in providing three different cords to draw them to himself! But how weakly do some men act, who suspend their faith, and hopes upon only one of them! By laying hold of them all, they would approach more speedily and certainly to the center of all happiness.

ADDITIONAL ARGUMENTS

To the arguments I have mentioned in favor of the use of the Bible as a schoolbook, I shall add a few reflections.

The present fashionable practice of rejecting the Bible from our schools, I suspect has originated with the deists. They discover great ingenuity in this new mode of attacking Christianity. If they proceed in it, they will do more in half a century, in extirpating our religion, than Bolingbroke or Voltaire could have effected in a thousand years. I am not writing to this class of people. I despair of changing the opinions of any of them. I wish only to alter the opinions and conduct of those lukewarm, or superstitious Christians, who have been misled by the deists upon this subject. On the ground of the good old custom, of using the Bible as a schoolbook, it becomes us to entrench our religion. It is the last bulwark the deists have left it; for they have rendered instruction in the principles of Christianity by the pulpit and the press, so unfashionable, that little good for many years seems to have been done by either of them.

The effects of the disuse of the Bible, as a schoolbook have appeared of late in the neglect and even contempt with which scripture names are treated by many people. It is because parents have not been early taught to know or respect the characters and exploits of the Old and New Testament worthies, that their names are exchanged for those of the modern kings of Europe, or of the principle characters in novels and romances. I conceive there may be some advantage in bearing scripture names. It may lead the persons who bear them, to study that part of the scriptures, in which their names are mentioned, with uncommon attention, and perhaps it may excite a desire in them to possess the talents or virtues of their ancient namesakes. This remark first occurred to me, upon hearing a pious woman whose name was Mary, say, that the first passages of the Bible, which made a serious impression on her mind, were those interesting chapters and verses in which the name of Mary is mentioned in the New Testament.

It is a singular fact, that while the names of the kings and emperors of Rome, are now given chiefly to horses and dogs, scripture names have hitherto been confined only to the human species. Let the enemies and contemners of those names take care, lest the names of more modern kings be given hereafter only to the same animals, and lest the names of the modern heroines of romances be given to animals of an inferior species.

It is with great pleasure, that I have observed the Bible to be the only book read in the Sunday schools in England. We have adopted the same practice in the Sunday schools, lately established in this city. This will give our religion (humanly speaking) the chance of a longer life in our country. We hear much of the persons educated in free schools in England, turning out well in the various walks of life. I have enquired into the cause of it, and have satisfied myself, that it is wholly to be ascribed to the general use of the Bible in those schools, for it seems the children of poor people are of too little consequence to be guarded from the supposed evils of reading the scriptures in early life, or in an unconsecrated school house.

However great the benefits of reading the scriptures in schools have been, I cannot help remarking, that these benefits might be much greater, did schoolmasters take more pains to explain them to their scholars. Did they demonstrate the divine original of the Bible from the purity, consistency, and benevolence of its doctrines and precepts-did they explain the meaning of the Levitical institutions, and show their application to the numerous and successive gospel dispensations-did they inform their pupils that the gross and abominable vices of the Jews were recorded only as proofs of the depravity of human nature, and of the insufficiency of the law, to produce moral virtue and thereby to establish the necessity and perfection of the gospel system-and above all, did they often enforce the discourses of our Savior, as the best rule of life, and the surest guide to happiness, how great would be the influence of our schools upon the order and prosperity of our country! Such a mode of instructing children in the Christian religion, would convey knowledge into their understandings, and would therefore be preferable to teaching them creeds, and catechisms, which too often convey, not knowledge, but words only, into their memories. I think I am not too sanguine in believing, that education, conducted in this manner, would, in the course of two generations, eradicate infidelity from among us, and render civil government scarcely necessary in our country.

In contemplating the political institutions of the United States, I lament, that we waste so much time and money in punishing crimes, and take so little pains to prevent them. We profess to be republicans, and yet we neglect the only means of establishing and perpetuating our republican forms of government, that is the universal education of our youth in the principles of Christianity, by means of the Bible; for this divine book, above all others, favors that equality among mankind, that respect for just laws, and all those sober and frugal virtues, which constitute the soul of republicanism.

I have now only to apologize for having addressed this letter to you, after having been assured by you, that your opinion, respecting the use of the Bible as a schoolbook, coincided with mine. My excuse for what I have done is, that I knew you were qualified by your knowledge, and disposed by your zeal in the cause of truth, to correct all the errors you would discover in my letter. Perhaps a further apology may be necessary for my having presumed to write upon a subject so much above my ordinary studies. My excuse for it is, that I thought a single mite from a member of a profession, which has been frequently charged with skepticism in religion, might attract the notice of persons who had often overlooked the more ample contributions upon this subject, of gentlemen of other professions. With great respect, I am, dear sir, your sincere friend.

BENJAMIN RUSH

Philadelphia, March 10, 1791

Influence of the Bible on Founders

A Brief Summary

The Founding Fathers did not believe that the Bible should be pushed to the margins of public life. Nor, was it the aspiration of only a handful of Founders to secure a place of prominence for the Bible and its teachings in American society. Rather, scholarly studies have shown that the Bible exercised the greatest literary influence over the whole of the Founding Fathers and their efforts to craft the government of their new nation.

The research of two scholars proves the formative influence accorded to the Bible by the Founding Fathers. Charles Hyneman was a distinguished professor of political science at Indiana University. Together with Donald S. Lutz, Associate Professor of Political Science at the University of Huston, these two professors reviewed an estimated 15,000 political documents from the founding era of America as an independent nation—an era of nearly half a century, extending from 1760 to 1805. Hyneman and Lutz published their findings in the early 1980s, and the results of their ten-year study were not kind to the fallacies of secularists and those seeking to exclude the Bible from public life. They showed that the single most often quoted source in the political writings of America's Founding Fathers was the Bible, which received 34% of the total number of quotes. Donald Lutz summarized their work in his book, *The Origins of American Constitutionalism*. Here Lutz called attention to the fact that the Bible exercised the greatest influence upon the thinking of the Founding Fathers and their formation of American government:

> The relative influence of European thinkers on American political thought is a large and complex question not to be answered in any but a provisional way here. We can, however, identify the broad trends of influence and which European thinkers need to be especially considered. One means to this end is an examination of the citations in public political literature written between 1760 and 1805. If we ask which book was most frequently cited in that literature, the answer is, the Bible.[13]

Quotations from additional sources did not receive near the attention accorded to the Bible by the Fathers. Baron Charles Montesquieu ranked a distant second with 8.3% of the total quotes, followed by British legal scholar, William Blackstone, at 7.9%, and theologian and political writer, John Locke, was quoted 2.9% of the time in the quotes identified by Hyneman and Lutz.[14] Further, it should be noted that most of the individuals the Founding Fathers quoted in the Hyneman-Lutz study were Christian thinkers and authors. For years, secularists have insisted that irreligious Enlightenment thinkers were the primary source of influence upon the Founding Fathers, but in fact, the radical Enlightenment thinkers had very little impact upon the development of American political life. One of the subsequent articles developed by Professor Lutz explained that the "First Enlightenment" thinkers were Christian and were credited with 16% of the political citations. The radical thinkers of the "Second Enlightenment," such as Voltaire, Diderot, and Helvetius, garnered only 2% of the citations while members of the "Third Enlightenment" era, typified by Rousseau, Mably, Raynal, and others, received a mere 4% of interest in the citations of the Founding Fathers.[15]

This study by two political science scholars clearly demonstrates the Founding Fathers' dependence upon the Bible for some of the most "innovative" principles that eventually made their way into the United States Constitution. And, what was the source of inspiration for these "innovations"? As was noted in some of their private writings, the Founding Fathers pointed to the Bible as their source of inspiration. In a letter to Thomas Jefferson, John Adams pointed to the general influence of the Christian faith upon the Fathers:

> The general principles on which the fathers achieved independence were the general principles of Christianity. I will avow that I then believed, and now believe, that those general principles of Christianity are as eternal and immutable as the existence and attributes of God. Without religion, this world would be something not fit to be mentioned in polite company...[16]

Dr. Rush and America's Founding Fathers knew that for America to survive and thrive it must operate out of deeply established spiritual and moral convictions, which could only be cultivated by the Word of God—the Bible. Contrary to the deception of secularists, America was not founded upon irreligion, but upon the principles of Christianity as revealed in the Bible. Alexis de Tocqueville was a French political thinker and historian who is best remembered for his famed work, *Democracy in America*, which he wrote after visiting America. He was concerned with why the secular French Revolution of his homeland had failed so miserably and why America's Revolution had been such an enormous success. After extensive travel in early-nineteenth-century America, he arrived at the conclusion that America was great because America was good. And, Dr. Rush would add, America is good because of the Gospel of Jesus Christ—as proclaimed in the Bible!

ENDNOTES

Notes and Sources

[1]"Massachusetts School Laws," Wikipedia, September 26, 2012; http://en.wikipedia.org/wiki/Massachusetts_School_Laws.

[2]Dumas Malone and et al, *Dictionary of American Biography*, s.v. "Girard, Stephen."

[3]Stephen Girard, *The Will of the Late Stephen Girard, Esq. Produced from the Office for the Probate of Wills, with a Short Biography of His Life* (Philadelphia: Thomas Desilver, 1848), 16.

[4]Girard, *Will of Stephen Girard*, 22-23.

[5]"Vidal V. Girard's Executors, 43 U.S. 127 (1844)," January 18, 2019; https://supreme.justia.com/cases/federal/us/43/127/.

[6]John Sanderson, *Biography of the Signers to the Declaration of Independence* (Philadelphia: R.W. Pomeroy, 1823), 4:285.

[7]Thomas Mitchell, and Philadelphia College of Medicine. *The Character of Rush: An Introductory to the Course on the Theory and Practice of Medicine, in the Philadelphia College of Medicine.* Philadelphia [Pa.]: John H. G, 4.

[8]David Ramsay, *A Eulogium Upon Benjamin Rush, M.D. Professor of the Institutes and Practice of Medicine and of Clinical Practice in the University of Pennsylvania Who Departed This Life April 19, 1813* [Philadelphia], 107.

[9]Dr. Rush was listed as one of two secretaries of the soci-

ety. See *Pennsylvania Society for Promoting the Abolition of Slavery. The Constitution of the Pennsylvania Society for Promoting the Abolition of Slavery, and the Relief of Free Negroes Unlawfully Held in Bondage Begun*, 7.

[10]*Pennsylvania Society for Promoting the Abolition of Slavery. Centennial Anniversary of the Pennsylvania Society, for Promoting the Abolition of Slavery, the Relief of Free Negroes Unlawfully Held in Bondage*, 14-15.

[11]*Journals of the Continental Congress, 1774-1789*. ed. Worthington C. Ford et al. Washington, D.C.: 1904., 1:26. See this entry online at http://memory.loc.gov/cgi-bin/query/r?ammem/hlaw:@field%28DOCID+@lit%28jc00110%29%29.

[12]Benjamin Rush, "A Defense of the Use of the Bible as a Schoolbook, Addressed to the Rev. Jeremy Belknap, of Boston," in *Essays, Literary, Moral and Philosophical by Benjamin Rush, M.D. And Professor of the Institutes of Medicine and Clinical Practice in the University of Pennsylvania* (Philadelphia: Thomas & Samuel Bradford, 1798), 93-113.

[13]Donald S. Lutz, *The Origin of American Constitutionalism* (Baton Rouge: Louisiana State University Press, 1988), 140.

[14]Lutz, *Origin of American Constitutionalism*, 139-147. Also see Charles S. Hyneman and Donald S. Lutz, *American Political Writing During the Founding Era, 1760-1805*, 2 vols. (Indianapolis: Liberty Press, 1983).

[15]Donald S. Lutz, "The Relative Influence of European Writers on Late Eighteenth-Century American Political Thought," *American Political Science Review* 189 (1984): 189-97.

[16]Original orthography updated. *The Papers of Thomas Jefferson*, vol. 6, *Retirement Series, 11 March to 27 November 1813* (Princeton: Princeton University Press, 209), 236-39.

Made in the USA
Middletown, DE
02 July 2023

34460644R10024